THE 3 YEAR REGRET AND 30K DEBT

IS UNIVERSITY THE RIGHT CHOICE FOR YOU?

JADE MARSH

© 2016 by Jade Marsh. All rights reserved.

No part of this book may be reproduced in any written, electronic, recording, or photocopying without written permission of the publisher or author. The exception would be in the case of brief quotations embodied in the critical articles or reviews and pages where permission is specifically granted by the publisher or author.

Although every precaution has been taken to verify the accuracy of the information contained herein, the author and publisher assume no responsibility for any errors or omissions. No liability is assumed for damages that may result from the use of information contained within.

Publisher: Jade Marsh

Visit the author's website at www.jademarsh.com

jade@jademarsh.com

ISBN-13: 978-1539333111
ISBN-10:1539333116

Contents

Preface ....

Introduction 1

Who is this book for? 2

My story and why you need to hear it 3

Do I need a degree? 22

Pros and Cons of going to University 33

21 Questions to ask yourself 45

Making a clear decision 77

What should I do instead of get a degree? 84

Finding your passion 100

The next step: Finding a mentor 111

Conclusion 123

Work with Jade 126

   Are you ready to create your dream lifestyle? 126

Preface

I thought it was necessary for me to write this book, as I was constantly coming in contact with people who had been to university, but were not working in a job related to their degree.

I also am not working from the efforts of my degree. In fact, I never worked in anything related. So, as for me, going to university was a mistake, a big one at that!

Time is precious, and so we must make the most of every second, minute, day, month, year we have. Wasting 3 precious years of my time taught me a big lesson!

The lesson was to always look at the pros and cons of every big decision I am about to make, do my research and to not rush into anything that requires such large time and monetary commitment.

This book will tell my story and try to give a fair discussion of the pros and cons of university.

My goal is to help, as many young people not make the same mistake I did, and to choose their next career path wisely with the guidance of this book.

I decided to write this book now, because I believe a lot of people can learn from my experience. I have found my calling in life, so I now feel it is time to help others find theirs quicker than I did.

Why should you listen to what I have to say? I have been there, done it, and got the t-shirt.

I had been searching for my passion since leaving high school 10 years ago. It was only recently I found it. I now know how you can find yours without taking as long as I did, and I am passionate about helping you.

Introduction

For people who have finished high school, one of the biggest decisions they will have to make is whether they should continue with higher education or to go straight into full time employment.

Each person will have their own judgement on whether university is, or isn't right for them. In my personal opinion, it is not necessary unless they absolutely have to obtain a degree in the profession they are looking to work in. Otherwise, I think it's a waste of time.

Why waste three or 4 years of being unproductive, when you could be out in the real world earning an income whilst you learn.

In this book, I will explain my story and give you a clear guide on the steps you need to take to make an informed decision on whether university is the next best step for you.

You will be asked a series of questions that you might not have ever asked yourself before, or given much thought, to help you make the best decision.

Who is this book for?

This book is aimed at young adults aged between 16-25 who are either looking into university straight from college, or for someone who has decided it could be an option for them when looking for a career change after working full time since school.

I believe that at such a young age with hardly any life experience, you're not capable of making a huge decision regarding the rest of your working life; therefore I don't agree that university is for everyone.

I am a big fan of it for the right person, but I believe a lot of people go and then regret it afterwards, and I can't see why people are making the same mistake over and over again when it could easily be avoided.

My story and why you need to hear it

I grew up in a small seaside town in Essex, UK, where there wasn't much opportunity for what I wanted to do.

My high school was average and I completed school with reasonable grades. Growing up, I had always known I wanted to be successful, which to me meant being financially free and doing something I loved.

When you are young, it's easy to assume you will get what you want when you grow up and become "rich" as I had said I wanted to be. As you get older, you realize that it's not as easy as that. You have actually got to figure out what you want to do, and genuinely be good at something; it doesn't just get handed to you on a plate.

I left school at 16 to do an apprenticeship in hairdressing as I had been offered a full time position after working as a Saturday girl for a year at a local hair salon.

Was it really what I wanted to do? No… I took on the job because I wanted to earn some real money and I was fed up of being in education.

I was the only one out of my group of friends that was working full time, as they had all stayed on to do their A-levels, which would prepare them for University.

I was earning £100 a week at the age of 16 while still living at home, so I thought I was doing pretty well at that time, considering all my friends had no money.

When I look back at that now, I realise I had always had an entrepreneur mind-set as I was always chasing the money, and I was prepared to do anything. I always worked hard.

After a few more years and a couple of hair salons later, I decided hairdressing wasn't for me anymore. It didn't pay nearly enough and I was bored of doing the same thing and being confined to one work environment.

What were my choices? Well I thought, "I better go to university."

Why? "Because isn't that what everyone does who wants to get into a good job and earn a decent living?"

I always had a dream of owning my own business but thought that was far away in the future and the first step I had to take was to go to university, gain a degree so I could be more employable…or so I thought.

So after the best summer of my life in Ibiza, I enrolled in a college to do a 1 year "access" course which would give me the equivalent to A-levels which I never did before I left school. This was necessary in order to be accepted into a university.

September 2011 soon came around, and I started university in London. I had enrolled onto an Events Management course, as I quite liked the idea of working in events. I saw myself as a party girl back then so thought this would suit me. I remember thinking I wasn't sure what course I really wanted to take, but events seemed like a good option at the time.

Half way through my first year, I combined two subjects so I ended up studying "Events Management, and Music Industry Management" By second year, I had dropped events to focus solely on Music Management as I thought to myself maybe I could be the next "Simon Cowell" yeah right! I had all these big ideas but no clue how I was going to achieve them. I was convincing myself of what I wanted. All I knew was I needed to be successful and earn a lot of money, I just didn't know how?

Third year of university came, and I was constantly being reminded by my lecturers, of how difficult it was to make money in the music industry. It really put me off and made me realise it was unlikely that I was going to be a huge success because I knew I had to be really passionate to make it work, and I just wasn't.

After graduating, I moved back to my home town and worked in my friend's café, which I'd done for a couple years on and off whilst studying. Whilst working there, I applied for jobs in London within the music industry to see what I was offered and then hopefully, figure out if it was really for me. I had just studied for 3 years so I decided to give it a shot so it wasn't a complete waste of time.

I had graduated at the age of 24. I went to university two years later than I should have done if I had gone straight from college like most people do. Some people might say that was a better idea as I was older and could appreciate it more, and I was wiser when it came to choosing my course. Wrong! I went to university because I got to a stage in life where I had no idea what I wanted and I panicked, so I thought going would be the answer. Most of my friends had taken the University route, so I felt like it was the right thing to do and I was going to walk into my dream job after graduating.

I believe that a lot of people are too young to make the huge decision to go to university. They haven't had enough life or work experience to figure out what they are truly passionate about and are forced to pick their course without knowing who they really are, or what they want to do for the rest of their life.

Although I had taken the time out, I still made the mistake of going when it wasn't right for me. I agree with taking time out if you're unsure, but I think that doing that alone isn't enough. It is important to seek advice from the right people and think about your options before taking on a 3-year commitment to do a degree.

I never had any work experience whilst I was studying for my degree, apart from a month at the "BBC" (The British Broadcasting Corporation) in the Events Department, which was no longer relevant for me after I had dropped events from my course.

Most of the jobs in the music industry that I came across were unpaid internships. To travel to London every day would have cost £600 a month, so it wasn't viable for me to get a job that was unpaid. I wasn't prepared to work for free at the age of 24 as I was looking to start saving to buy my own house.

The starting salary for graduate jobs outside of the music industry started at around £18,000- £20,000 if you were lucky. After taking travel costs and tax out of that salary, it wasn't going to leave me with much left over each month, to save for a house.

I was feeling very deflated at how many years it would take me to build up my dream income.

I didn't have years, as I wanted it immediately. I also didn't want to travel to London every day, which would have taken 4 hours on the train. I thought to myself "There must be more to life than this". After growing up excited that I was going to make a big success of myself, reality hit me hard. I had big expectations and by that point I was feeling like maybe it wasn't going to happen for me and I should just settle for an average life.

I thought, "Okay, I'll go down the PA (personal assistant) route," because that paid quite well. For six months, I had been applying for jobs but I wasn't even offered an interview. I now know why, because my heart wasn't in it; I knew that I didn't want to work in London. I yearned for something else.

It was then I was introduced to Network Marketing through a friend, and that is when everything changed. Network marketing gives the average person the opportunity to start their own business under the umbrella of a global company; in this case it was a health and wellness company. It is similar to a franchise but much cheaper. I paid £200 to start my business, entering into a partnership with my sister. Initially, the idea was to earn an income whilst I was seeking employment in London.

A couple of months into the business, I realized the potential of what people were achieving, so I decided this was going to be my career and I was going to make it work no matter what.

I was introduced to the world of entrepreneurship and it also really turned me off working for someone else. My eyes were opened up to what a traditional job entailed, and it looked like hell to me!

The average person works 45 years of their life, for what? To survive…to pay the bills and to get by. Then they come to an age where they can retire and struggle some more. By this time, their health is starting to deteriorate to the point where they can't really enjoy life anyway. I hear a lot of people saying, "I'll do this and that when I retire", why not do it now? Why wait until then? You might not even make it to retirement age… harsh but true!

If you aren't doing anything meaningful then you are just working your life away…what is the point?

I have always been career minded, and seen myself doing something, which I love that is a big part of my life, not just something that pays the bills. I wouldn't be content with just getting married and having children, a career is just as important to me. Previous employers have always praised me for how ambitious I was. To not be successful was never an option for me.

I never felt like I had found my true self, because I was chasing this dream even though I wasn't sure what it was at the time.

I wanted more of a purpose; life can get boring if you don't have something that keeps you motivated and driven. I think a career plays a major part in living a fulfilled life as it gives you an identity.

You spend most of your life working, so why not do something you love, which you would be excited to get out of bed for. I wanted something that I was passionate about and I was trying to find it in Network Marketing.

When you're young, your excited to enter the real world and work, then maybe 10 years in, your bored and your thinking, "Is this it?" There must be more to life than working. I saw the result of this at my Network Marketing company events, from meeting new people who were desperate to leave their full time jobs to be in control of their work life.

The majority of people would love to have the opportunity to travel the world, be their own boss and be financially independent. Most people aren't prepared to put the hard graft in for a few years so they can live the rest of their life how they choose to.

After building our business for 18 months, my sister and I hit a brick wall; we became less focused and lost belief in ourselves, along with our drive and passion for what we were doing. I wasn't enjoying it anymore, and when I look back now, I think it was because I was chasing the money, rather than actually doing something I was truly passionate about.

I was searching for something different but I didn't know what? Network Marketing was all I had known for the last 18 months, so I was scared to make a change and hoped I would get my motivation back again.

I had been following a lady *Danelle Delgado* on Facebook for around 6 months. She had been successful in Network Marketing previously, but was now a coach for entrepreneurs.

I saw Danelle was promoting a retreat online which was being held in St. Marten, in the Caribbean. It was for entrepreneurs looking to take their business to the next level. I knew I had to attend. It was what I had been looking for, something was calling me and after speaking to Danelle over Skype, I knew it was going to be life changing.

I was directed into coaching whilst being on the retreat as they saw I was passionate about helping people, particularly those that were deciding on whether to go to university or not, like I had been 5 years ago. I regretted going and wished I had made better choices. I saw this as an opportunity for me to guide people so they didn't make the same mistake that I did.

I felt so strongly about it, that anyone I came into contact with who was planning to attend university to do something similar to what I did. I would advise them against it and suggest another option for them.

I believe that going to university is one of the biggest mistakes that people can make early on in their career. I would always encourage people to start making money from a young age by starting work as early as they can, depending on what type of career they wanted.

For most people, the goal is to work hard when they are young, so they can retire early right? For me, I have never wanted that. I have always wanted to be financially free by a young age, but never wanted to retire and do nothing.

My aim has always been to have a career that will allow me to work into my old age. I believe your career is what makes you who you are, so why would you give that up? It's like giving up a part of you, and you were put on this earth to make a difference, so why stop when you have made a lot of money?

If you find out what your true passion in life is, then it won't feel like work, because you will love what you do. That is the ultimate goal and should be what everyone aims for. We all deserve to be doing what we desire and to be excited by life, rather than our work sucking the life out of us.

I believe MONEY and Health are two of the biggest stressors in life...

We can take control of our financial situation, but we only have some control over our health. So why wouldn't we want to illuminate our worry over money, as that is the one thing we can have full control over.

Of course, I am not saying money is everything and that everyone should become millionaires. What I am saying is, wouldn't you want to secure your future just a little bit better? So, you have more time to do the things you want to do in life.

I feel that most people put limitations on themselves due to what they have been fed through society, education, their families beliefs, past experiences, or how they were raised.

The truth is there are more opportunities out there than we know, just that most of us are walking around blind to them, as we don't believe we have any other choice.

If you aren't happy in your chosen career, then change it. Find an opportunity that will suit you better, and don't stop searching until you find the one that does.

The difference between an average person and a successful person, is that a successful person is walking around with their eyes open, rather than closed. They are searching and waiting for the next big opportunity to be presented to them as they are open minded enough to take a look, and they want to live a better quality of life than most people.

I think a lot of people feel stuck, that they don't have a choice, they have been dealt the life they have been given, and they should just get on with it and make the most out of it.

We can be anyone we want to be or do anything we want to do. First of all, we need to believe, educate ourselves, and then take action.

The biggest thing I learned from starting my own business was the importance of personal development. It is something I knew very little about. I had read the book "The Secret" but that was about as far as my personal development had gone.

Everyone should aim to develop him or herself personally, on a daily basis even if they aren't building a business. Why this isn't taught at school is beyond me, as it has been the pinnacle reason for me starting my own business.

Had I invested in personal development from a young age, I would have achieved success a lot quicker than I did, I am 100% sure of it. Without developing yourself mentally, how do you expect to get anywhere far in life? I believe this needs to be taught in schools as I think it would have a huge impact on kids positively at a young age.

We put limitations on ourselves, parents, teachers, friends, employers, and work colleagues also put limitations on us. The only thing holding us back is ourselves, and working on our mind set daily can be life changing to say the least.

The amount of negativity I received from joining a network marketing company was unbelievable; from people close to me and people I didn't know. You find out who your true friends are when you go against the "norm" of what the majority are doing.

Most people are like sheep and they follow what the average person is doing because it's safe. If you want an average life, keep following the average people. If you want more, then do the opposite to the rest.

The biggest investment you can make is in yourself, and yet people are less likely to spend money on improving their mental well-being as they do their physical appearance. If only they knew the huge benefits it could have on their life in the long run.

A lot of people look at successful people and tell themselves, "They are lucky" and completely overlook what they did in order to get there. I think people do this because it makes them feel better about what they haven't achieved.

No one becomes successful overnight, it's just that we don't see all the pain and failure that they went through.

Being an entrepreneur isn't easy. In fact, it's really hard, probably one of the hardest things you will do… Why? Because it takes time, persistence, a good mental attitude to succeed and to constantly pick yourself up again, when you fail.

Although it isn't easy, neither is working for someone else. Most people would choose to be in control of their work life, wouldn't they?

A lot of people haven't got the confidence to go after what they want as they are scared to fail which I totally understand. On a daily basis, I ask myself, "Can I do this?"

"Is this really for me?" Because I get scared and I wonder if I am meant for big things, but I know I don't have a choice as I refuse to live an average life, and if I never achieve what I wanted to, at least I spent my life trying.

The reason for me writing this book is so I can help my former self 5 years ago… I wish I had someone who guided and mentored me so I could have chosen the right path. I was not in the right position to make the best decision for myself when I chose to attend university. I never gave it a proper thought because I had no one to show me the pros and cons and what my other options were.

It was a lazy way out of a situation I wasn't happy in, and I feel there are a lot of young adults who waste a lot of time doing the wrong things or working in the wrong job for years because they haven't been educated on what is out there.

Of course, it all starts with personal development. This should be presented to you as soon as you can read a book. It will develop you mentally and emotionally in a more positive way than anything you see on the television or read in the paper.

Going to university was a huge regret of mine. I hate wasting time, it's one of my biggest pet hates; I value life and the short time we are here. I love experiencing new things and meeting new people, so I don't regret that part. It's not even the amount I spent that I regret so much, although I am largely motivated by money, so the thought of what I could have earned in those 3 years pains me.

Rather, I regret the time I wasted doing nothing productive (in my eyes), being taught something that wasn't in line with my passion. I will never get those 3 years back.

I have accepted that I went when I didn't need to, but I no longer dwell on it, as I understand why I took that path. I took it because I am where I am today writing this book in the hope I make a difference to people. I want to stop as many young people as I can from making the same mistake as I did.

I had to make that mistake in order to educate others not to do the same. It is now my mission and my goal to help other people, and if I could help just one person realise their true potential and passion in life and give them the confidence to pursue it; rather than follow suit and do what everyone else does, then this book will have served its purpose and I will be extremely happy!

I also want to make it clear to you that living in regret is not a good thing to do, as it can hold you back. It is something that I have learned to overcome as we all have regrets. You may be reading this thinking that you don't have a big regret just yet, but it's likely you will have at least one in your life.

Don't regret anything in life as you did what you thought was right at the time given the information or situation you were in. How could you possibly know how it was going to affect you in the future?

I am not anti- university, so please do not misunderstand the message I am trying to portray throughout this book. I am against it for certain people and looking back, I am against it for my former self. It is a great option for people who know exactly what they want to do and are going into a job that requires special skills and training.

Having said that, the aim of this book is to encourage the next generation entrepreneurs not to waste their time at university, and also to help anyone else who is debating on going, to look at the all facts and really think about the future from their point of view, no one else's.

People are making misinformed decisions, which is costing them time and money when it could have easily been avoided. My goal is stop that from happening and to enlighten people in making the best decision based on their dreams and ambitions.

Hopefully, I can be that guidance for you and help you figure it out…

CHAPTER 1

Do I need a degree?

It isn't about whether you need a degree; it's about whether the job you want to apply for, asks for one.

Before you decide on University as an option for you, of course you need to know whether you need a degree for what it is you want to do, career wise. Not everyone needs one, and in this book, I will explore why I believe most people don't actually need a degree in today's world unless it is absolutely mandatory which most of us are led to believe.

Creative industries most likely will ask for a degree, but realistically, you don't need one, you just need to show your creative side and find someone that will hire you, which they will if you're confident and persistent, and allow yourself to stand out from the crowd.

If you do go to University to get a degree for the creative industry, then it is likely you will have to intern unpaid for a few months, and it isn't guaranteed you will be offered a job. So if that is the case, I believe the better option would be to work unpaid for a short period of time until you do get offered a job, as this will take less time than studying for a degree.

My University never had the resources to help when it came to finding work experience, or a job for that matter, which is something I expected help with.

I was sure they would have some great connections, but unless one of the lecturers knew anyone in the music industry, I was pretty much left to find work for myself. I am not saying this is a bad thing, as ultimately it's up to you to make your own way in life, I am just clarifying how unhelpful going to University was for me.

Universities would offer more value, if they helped you find work whilst you are studying. Qualifications alone don't get you a job; you would be more successful with qualifications and experience combined.

It is difficult when you're looking for a job yourself as most companies ask for experience, which you can't get if no one will give you a chance; it's a vicious circle. If you had the university's support when applying for jobs, it would make the process a lot easier.

I was never an academic, so it never made sense for me to go to university. Why would I go back into 3 years of education? When I am a more proactive person. I learn better by doing the job, not by someone standing in front of me explaining to me how it works. I believe that's the biggest thing that's missing from universities is hands on experience.

I am a practical learner anyway, so I can sit in lectures and be taught all there is to know about the music industry, do I remember a lot of it? No… Why? Because unless I am putting it into practice every day, then it's likely I will forget it. I learn best when I am doing something.

It all comes down to what type of learner you are; I go into detail about this in chapter 6.

Being pro-active is what gets you the results. You

could be a straight A student but if you're not actually going to go out and do the work, then you are never going to be successful. Yes, you will be successful at taking exams and writing essays, but you're never going to make it in the real world if you don't take action.

Having a degree versus not having a degree

Going to university is great if you're not quite ready to get stuck into a job, but if your someone who is highly self-motivated, willing to work, and who uses their initiative, then I don't believe formal education is for you. You know what type of person you are and what you are capable of. Although university can be important, what matters the most is skills, and you learn the best when you're actually doing the job.

If you are applying for a job with say 100 other people, and 50 of you have a degree, then of course you will be moved to the top of the pile and be more of a priority. Still that doesn't mean you need a degree, it just means you need to be incredibly driven and more creative when it comes to building your personal brand and attracting an employer's attention.

Most highly paid jobs will ask for a degree, but only to filter out the masses of people who apply. They are looking for good quality people who can commit themselves for a long period of time, who are loyal enough and passionate enough to do a good job for them. You can have all those qualities without a degree.

Yes, you will find statistics that state that people with a degree do earn more than those who don't, but statistics also say that half of UK graduates are stuck in jobs that don't require a degree.

The graduates that do earn more are typically the ones in jobs that require a specialised degree any way, which is realistic as specific skills and training is required.

If you were born an ambitious individual, then nothing will stop you from obtaining your dream job. You don't need to get a degree to make connections and work your way up in a high-powered job; you can do that without attending university for 3 years.

When you are young, especially if you have just come out of high school, you aren't in the position to make the best decision based on your career, instead you are being encouraged by older siblings, friends, parents, teachers that the next best step for you is university when it isn't always, or in most cases, your only option.

After spending 3-4 years studying for a degree, you are then forced into a job, which you probably could have acquired without your degree.

When do I need a degree?

Needing a degree is 100% industry dependent. If you are looking to commit your life to being a doctor, which I think is a life calling, it's likely you won't change your career. It's for life, considering it will take you 5-7 years to complete a medical degree.

If you are interested in law, science, engineering, medical training, mathematics, then it is necessary to either earn a degree, or a degree and then a PHD. Once you have researched into your options, you will know what is required for what exactly it is you want to do, then you can decide the appropriate steps to take.

The most successful entrepreneurs never went to university or have many qualifications for that matter.

Reasons for going to university:

- Higher education
- A requirement for working in a specific industry
- You're interested in studying a subject in a more depth manner
- Gaining transferable skills
- Higher job satisfaction

The truth about finding a job:

More than half of UK graduates are in non-graduate jobs due to lack of finding one, lack of experience, or because they aren't interested in what they studied anymore. More people are going to university now, therefore there aren't enough high skilled jobs to match the number of graduates.

The government has estimated that 45% of graduates will not earn enough to repay their student loans.

Let's take a look at some of the most successful people and see how education played a part or didn't play a part in their success.

Simon Cowell:

The music mogul dropped out of school at age 16 and was in and out of jobs until he started working in the mailroom at the music publishers his dad worked at. From there, he started his own independent label, which after some short-lived success, failed.

Cowell then climbed the corporate ladder at BMI and the rest is history! Simon Cowell is now known worldwide as one of the most successful entrepreneurs in music and is worth an estimated £325 million. Not bad for dropping out of school at age 16.

Richard Branson:

Richard left school at 16 as he struggled with dyslexia and was a poor student academically. His teacher told him that he would either end up in prison or become a millionaire.

Branson today is known as the founder of one of the biggest brands on the planet *Virgin* which, now consists of more than 200 companies worldwide. He has a record label, an airline, train-company, a luxury game preserve, a mobile phone company and a space-tourism company. He is estimated to be worth a whopping $5.1 billion.

Sir Jack Cohen:

The owner of Britain's biggest supermarket *Tesco* started out with a market stall, selling groceries in east London in 1919. Ten years later, Tesco's first store was opened. Tesco became a market leader and was the world's fourth biggest retailer.

University wasn't for me as I have always been entrepreneurial minded, so if you are also, then I would never recommend going. Rather, figure out what your passion is and go from there. Higher education was never meant for everyone; so don't feel like it has to be the next step for you.

Young people are being sold a dream that if they get a degree, then the world is their oyster. After 3 years of study, they still haven't found their passion and are left with a worthless piece of paper and huge debts, while missing out on earning an income for 3 years.

Having a degree might be beneficial in the way that you can get a higher paid job, but most likely, you will be working long hours. You will be doing this for 30-40 years, does it sound like a great option now?

This is why you have to really think about where you want to be in the long run. You might think you want a job working for someone else, but if you're looking for time and financial freedom, then that probably isn't the best option for you.

I got into debt and wasted 3 years for what? Yes, I made some great friends, I gained some life experience from living away from home in London, but it didn't set me up for my career. In fact it actually held me back from starting one.

If you decide to attend university, it has to be for the right reasons, not just because you have been told to go or you think it's the next step. Do your research!!

It isn't about what school, college or university you went to, it's about your unique talent and skillset. It is your job to show employers your innate abilities, as that is what employers are really looking for.

I believe employers are shifting towards a greater focus on raw potential these days and are looking for people with key skills, rather than people with just a degree.

Do you really need a degree for what you want to do? If yes, then great! You know exactly what direction your heading in.

If no, then don't just go to university for the sake of going. In the following chapters, I will help you decide where you go from here if you're still contemplating your next step.

CHAPTER 2

Pros and Cons of going to University

Before you can make a clear judgement on whether University is for you, it's important to get yourself familiar with its pros and cons, to help you make an informed decision.

University can offer you some major advantages, but it can also offer some major disadvantages. Academic life isn't for everyone, and the assumption that it is, is unfair to young people and puts expectations on them, which can force them into taking on the commitment of going when it isn't the best option for them.

I think that a lot of people study any subject, just for the sake of gaining a degree.

How do I know that? Because it's exactly what I did!

A degree is pointless if it isn't related to a subject that you love and see yourself using to build a career. Having said that, it can be a great choice for someone with the right mind-set.

Do you know what your next step is in your career path? It really depends on what you are looking for and you need to weigh your options, based on what is best for you and no one else.

The best way to do that is to compare the pros and cons to see which ones best suit you.

Pros:

- You will make lifelong friends
- Endless parties
- Create a whole new social circle
- Learning new skills
- Gaining a degree and adding more credibility to your CV
- Life experience
- Learn to become more independent
- Staying educated
- Find out more about yourself
- Degrees are respected
- You will study in depth a subject which interests you
- Graduates stand a better chance of getting a good job
- Many jobs require a degree today
- Graduates can earn more

Cons:

- Getting into debt- fees of up to £9,000 per year and the cost of living estimated around £4,500 per year depending on where you live, cities will be double at least
- A degree takes 3-4 years
- Won't earn a full time salary for at least 3-4 years whilst studying
- Find it difficult to enter the real world of working after being a student for so long, prolonging a student mentality
- No guarantee of a good job when you leave
- Work load- higher level amount of work compared to A-levels
- Degree's aren't everything, experience speaks larger volumes these days
- So much free online content you can teach yourself almost anything
- Not all graduates get well-paid jobs
- Some non-graduates become extremely successful
- If you choose the wrong degree, or after you graduate you are no longer interested in what you studied, you would have wasted 3 years and have racked up huge debts
- Missing out on opportunities due to being committed to the 3-4-year course
- Delaying the chance to be productive and becoming successful

- Jobs that require degrees are disappearing
- University doesn't prepare you for the real world
- Not all 18 year olds are ready for university

My Pros:

- Made me realize what I actually wanted in life
- Met some great people
- Was an experience
- I have a degree that I may use in the future (although I highly doubt it)
- Gave me the purpose to write this book and help people similar to me

My Cons:

- Wasted 3 years of my life that I will never get back
- Spent £30K
- Did a course that I wasn't passionate about, therefore was no longer interested in it when I graduated
- I didn't need university for what I wanted to do
- The work load
- Not being able to walk straight into a job
- Not given any support in finding work experience

- Not earning a decent income for 3 years
- I hated being a student
- I am driven by money, not qualifications
- I am an **entrepreneur** not an **academic**

Testimonials:

Anna (Teacher) studied English and American literature and Drama:

I personally think university is a great idea, because I am a believer in education for the sake of education and that it provides an opportunity to study something that you enjoy; I don't believe in the idea that you have to know what you want to do at the end of it because I certainly didn't.

I had a great time and loved studying, and so I just went ahead to further my education. I had no idea what I wanted to do and I didn't train to be a teacher until 5 years ago, but I wouldn't have been able to, if I didn't have a degree in the first place.

If you know what you want to do and choose a course from the beginning, something like medicine for example, then that is great. However, there are so many young people with brilliant minds who don't know where they want to go, that it is another string they can add to their bow whilst they are deciding.

Alex (Entrepreneur) Studied Fashion Design, Styling and Promotion:

I completed my a levels and then went on to do an art foundation course where I originally decided I wanted to take a degree in fashion. However during my art foundation I was highly persuaded to start a new course at Middlesex university which was known as "Fashion Design, Styling and Promotion" This seemed an ok title as I was keeping in all 3 areas I was interested in but ultimately I wanted to focus my life on design!

A year in and I was unsure why I had been persuaded to take a course, which involved absolutely no design, I was disheartened and told it was the first year this course had been running so I continued on hoping it would get better.

By second year when we was due to start work experience my really arrogant awful tutor told us university would get us nowhere, it was basically a waste of time, what we needed was industry experience. I couldn't believe my eyes, had I really just wasted 2 years of my life and accumulated unnecessary debt? Yes it would seem but I only had 1 more year to go and I wasn't a quitter!! We had no help whatsoever in finding a placement and considering all of our tutors were from the "so called industry" not one of them could put us forward for an interesting role to gain experience!!

My opinion of university is that it isn't needed in something like this, experience out weighs coursework and I could have spent 3 years travelling around London working for top designers, instead I was falsely led into a course that was absolutely thrown together and of not much value. My advice, if you are completing an academic course for an academic career then go for it, if your not and your career path is industry based then keep knocking on those doors and be persistent! That will serve you well, not endless amounts of debt!

Juliana (Litigation Paralegal) Studied Law:

I completely agree that a university degree will not be a pass to a perfect career. University is not for everyone and not all career paths require it. For the career path I have chosen, university is the only route.

To become a lawyer, there is practically a checklist of qualifications you need (and even then, it was extremely hard). Students wanting to study law will spend a lengthy time studying and then paying for LPC/BPTC as funding is very rare. Those wanting to become lawyers need to become more realistic about the career prospects and the length of the process. This is something I was not made aware off and was actually demoralised for a while.

My desire for law kept me going and I'm now working as a paralegal - the costs of doing the LPC / BPTC is not something I can afford, so I would say I'm rather behind my peers who are training now, after finding it themselves.

Tony (Junior A+R) Studied Music Industry Management:

I feel like I am one of the few graduates I know that has a university degree relative to their career. However, it wasn't always as straightforward. University was especially hard having taken a year of leave the year I was formally supposed to enter university. Having exited my first lecture, the words resounding in my head were '3 years of this? I don't think so'.

As time elapsed I began to grow into my course and it was intriguing how I began to start looking at Music from a different angle; the dark and hidden (yet indispensable) knowledge that was needed in order to survive the business. Though valuable knowledge-wise, I cannot convincingly say that the experience as a whole was 3 years of fireworks and rainbows. It was particularly shameful that the most relevant module to my course was the last module of the final year!! To conclude, my personal opinion: attend university if you know what you want to do, not to find what you want to do

I was never passionate about the course I was doing. I think I tried to convince myself I was, but deep down I knew my heart wasn't in it, and as I came to the end of my degree, doubts starting kicking in about why I had gone to university in the first place.

The pros and cons will be personal to you, one pro for someone might be a con for another, it really depends on what you would be going to university for and what you hope to achieve from it.

By weighing up the pros and cons, it might be possible for you to immediately identify what option is best for you. I would also suggest rating each pro and con on a scale of 1-10, with 10 being the most important, and 1 being the least important. This will allow you to see how important each pro and con are to you and how much each one will affect you in the long run.

You may still feel unsure after doing this exercise. If that is the case, re-visit it on another day. The next chapter will help you delve deeper into how you truly feel. Your 'gut feeling' or intuition will be a strong indicator on whether you are making the right decision based on your core values and what is best for you.

CHAPTER 3

21 Questions to ask yourself

Now you have looked at the pros and cons, it's important to ask yourself some vital questions to evaluate everything and have some clear answers of how you feel about going to university. It is a huge decision, and for most, it's the first big decision they will make as an adult and it will have the biggest impact on the start of their career.

Going to university means something different for everyone. For some, it's a tradition in one's family, so it is almost expected they go. For others, they might be the first person in their family to ever consider or have the opportunity to go, therefore their parents are all for it. What parent doesn't want their children to have the best start in life? As mentioned before, it is only the best start for the right person. Remember, this is your decision based on how you feel.

For some, it's more about the experience, and going for the party lifestyle students are known for. Waking up late, partying too hard, living away from home and having your own independence, rather than going for the actual degree.

Whatever the reason, it is individual to you, so before committing 3 years of your life and taking on a huge loan, its important you have really given it considerable thought.

Therefore, the decision shouldn't be made lightly. It's important to ask yourself the appropriate questions, before making up your mind.

Ask yourself these 21 questions and write down your answers without giving it too much thought. Just write down what first comes to mind, without overthinking them or answering them how you feel you should, you might be surprised!

1. What is university like?

University is a different experience for everyone. I went to university in London, so I don't think you get the whole party experience there that you can get at a smaller campus.

I also went a little older than a lot of people, so I didn't feel the need to go out partying all the time.

It is up to you to make it a memorable experience and get as much out of it as you can, a situation is only as good as you make it.

The idea is to study hard, come away with the highest degree class you can, make as many connections as possible, get work experience, become more independent, learn like skills, make lifelong friends and of course, have some fun!

2. Why would I consider going?

I can imagine there are a lot of students who just assume that going to university is for them, as there is a misconception that it is a requirement in order to land a great job. You need to stop and consider whether it is right for you before you rush into making the decision to go.

My heart wasn't in it when I went, as I only chose to go because it was what everyone else was doing. I never really stopped and thought about whether it was actually for me or not.

Really think about the number one reason you would go, how will it benefit you and in what way?

You should consider going if you are interested in a particular career and you need a degree for that chosen career. There are only certain jobs you actually need a degree for.

3. Do I know what I would want to study?

You need to have a general idea of what you want to study, so you can look into universities that offer something that relates to your interests and desired subject.

Choose the course you want to undertake and then choose your desired university based on that. It is always wise to have more than one option in case you don't get accepted into your first choice.

There is no point picking a university for the location it is in. You have to make sure it actually meets your requirements and the course is a reputable one.

Make sure you choose something that will be of benefit to you when looking for a job. If you don't know what you want to do yet, then choose something that you are interested in learning more about. If you do know what you want to do, then you need to study a course that will meet the requirements of the job your looking to go into.

It is important to choose a course that you feel passionate about and can truly commit time to. Having said that, you are able to change your course if it is something you are not sure about after you have been studying it for a while.

You should have a general idea of what you hope to achieve and what you want to do when you finish. It is likely it will change a couple of times throughout your course as you become more knowledgeable and find your way, but it's important to have a guideline so you're not studying for a degree that becomes irrelevant to your career when you graduate, else it will be a waste of time like it was for me.

You don't just want to enroll on any course that sounds like something you might like, just so you get the chance to go. It is a huge commitment and what you choose to study is the main reason you're going. It has to be something you're at least interested in, and preferably, one that will assist you in your career when you graduate.

Having said that, it is possible to add another subject or drop a subject if you are looking to combine two subjects like I did and do a joint honor's degree. Although it is possible to switch courses, it's not always straightforward, so you are better off putting the time in now to research the hell out of it rather than getting there and trying to change it.

You will have to check with the University you are applying for, on how easy it is to change your course when you are there, in case it turns out to be nothing like you expected. Make sure you do your research into what university best suits the course you want to do as some specialize in certain topics, so one might suit you better than the other.

It also depends on the type of programme you wish to change, as to whether it is feasible and if there is space on the course you wish to change to, and when you decide to change. If it is half way through the year, and you have missed some mandatory modules on the course you want to change to, you might not have time to catch up and complete the work for that year.

Remember you will be studying your chosen subject for the next three years, so make sure it's something that will keep you interested and you have the ability to complete.

A lot can change in the time it takes to complete your degree; you can change your mind, and also after studying something for so long, a lot of people are fed up with it and decide it isn't for them after all. You will also do a lot of growing up in the time you are at university, which will make you look at things differently also.

4. What is my end goal?

Think about when you leave university and what you hope to do. Are you looking to go straight into a job? Will you be looking to move to another country or go travelling?

Although this might be hard, as it's hard enough knowing what you want to do in life now, let alone in 3 years' time after you have done something you haven't even experienced yet or know nothing about.

Always have a plan, otherwise you will be wandering around aimlessly in life and before you know it, you will be 65 and look back, thinking, "What the hell did I do with my life". You need to have an idea of where you want to end up; it doesn't mean you are always going to stick to the plan. In fact, it's likely your plan will change all the time. This is normal and its ok, as long as you have a guideline to run along while you try and figure your future out. Opportunities arise all the time and they present themselves when we least expect it, but always be ready and open to trying new things.

"If you fail to plan, you are planning to fail!"- Benjamin Franklin

Depending on what you decide to do, at least decide where you expect to work. For example, you may have to work in a city in order to get the job you hope for, so it would be wise to go to a university in that city, so you can access work experience whilst studying and you will get used to living there, plus make connections and network with people that can help you, for when you graduate.

"It's not what you know, it's who you know"

The decision you are thinking of making, does it align with your end goal? Is it going to get you to where you want to be? If you are unsure, seek out someone who can help you; someone who can advise you on the best option you need to take, depending on what it is you're interested in doing as a career.

5. What job do I hope to get?

Deciding the type of career you want is really important when deciding whether university is for you, as this will help you decide on your course and whether you should be going to university in the first place.

Are you looking for a high-powered career? What motivates and drives you?

For some of you, you may not be looking for a career, you might just be looking to do something to pay the bills, and that's ok if that's what you decide, but then maybe you shouldn't be contemplating university at all, unless you are looking to go for the experience, and if you're ok with studying for another three years.

What you want to do after is an indication of whether a degree is necessary for you or not.

6. Is it necessary to get a degree for what I want to do?

For some jobs, a degree isn't necessary, for others it is. I am going to explain what jobs require one and what jobs don't, to the best of my ability.

Most jobs, especially in the creative industries experience stands out a lot more than a qualification. There are so many online courses you can do now; let's say for instance you wanted to be a fashion designer. Most jobs will ask for a degree for this, so are you going to wait 3 years to learn how to design clothes, or are you going to teach yourself? Go on smaller courses, which are shorter than 3 years and a hell of a lot cheaper.

If I knew what I know now, and I wanted to be a fashion designer… I would teach myself how to make clothes, or at least design them. I would then make a collection of clothing and apply for jobs and show them what I could do. I guarantee you, they will take me over someone with a degree, and especially if I have taken it upon myself to teach myself everything I need to know.

I plan to start my own fashion line within the next couple of years. Have I got a degree no? Do I know anything about starting one, not really but that's why we have the Internet! It's opened up so many doors for us. Also the power of networking with people, who have already done it, is key.

Just because I don't really know how to get started, I mean I have some idea as I know how to build a business it's all generic, but because I have an entrepreneur mind-set, I would rather teach myself as its quicker and cheaper.

TIME IS MONEY… remember that! You can't get time back; don't wait until you are a professional at something, before you start.

Start now and learn as you go… I hear people say all the time, I am going back to university to learn how to do so and so and then eventually, I want to start my own business in it, but first I need experience. How about you go get some experience or just start your business around a full time job until you are able to leave that full time job. You can Google pretty much anything these days: how to set up an events company, how to be a fashion designer etc. There is so much free value and content online, it's ridiculous! Wouldn't you rather teach yourself? You can seek advice in a mentor, than go and sit in a classroom and pay at least 30k for the pleasure.

7. What jobs require a degree?

According to Forbes, here are 10 of the most sought after jobs that require a university/college degree:

- Marketing Executive
- Software Developer
- Registered Nurse
- Industrial Engineer
- Network and Computer System Administrator
- Web Developer- high level in a company
- Medical and Health Services Manager
- Physical Therapist
- Speech-Language Pathologist

To add to that list: Doctor, Dentist, Hygienist, Physiotherapist, Psychologist, Lawyer, any form of engineering jobs, Financial Analyst, Forensic Scientist, criminologists, teaching are all jobs that require a degree. I have most likely missed some out, but you get the idea. Jobs that are specialized will always require training that is of a degree standard.

19 leading jobs, which require no university degree:

Jobs	Average Income
1. Online Advertising manager	£66,000
2. Web Developer- starting your company or freelancing	£58,000
3. Medical Secretary	£23,000
4. Paralegal Assistant	£35,000
5. Stenographer-court Reporter	£36,000
6. Heating and Refrigeration Mechanic	£32,000
7. Surveyor	£42,000
8. Executive Assistant	£33,000
9. Insurance Agent	£35,000
10. Industrial Machine Repairer	£34,000
11. Cosmetologist	£17,000

12. Hair Stylist	£17,000
13. Tax Examiner-Collector	£37,000
14. Wholesales sales representative	£39,000
15. Construction machine operator	£30,000
16. Electrical Technician	£42,000
17. Architectural Drafter	£35,000
18. Teacher's Aide	£17,000
19. Sewage Plant Operator	£31,000

8. Am I going for the right reasons?

Whether you are thinking of going to university, or thinking of not going, are you thinking that way for the right reasons? Don't be pressured into a decision, you have to make sure whatever you decide; it's for you and no one else.

A lot of parents like the idea of their kids going to university, especially if they didn't go themselves. Nevertheless, it's really up to you and you need to be sure that you're going for the right intentions. You shouldn't be going if you're unsure of what you want and you are just trying to buy yourself some time to figure out what you want, as you will regret it after.

9. Am I committed to another 3-4 years of study?

It is likely you have just finished college and are looking to go straight into university. A lot of people are sick and tired of learning and are ready to get out into the world of work and start earning a wage, or there are some people who would prefer to be a student for as long as possible.

It is important to be constantly learning throughout life, but you can earn whilst you are learning, in most cases. Whilst at university, it is a good idea to get as much work experience as you can, but in most cases, it will be unpaid.

10. How much will it cost me?

Have you looked into how much it will cost to go to university? There are the tuition fees to take into account, the cost of living if you are moving away from home. It is a good idea to see how much rent costs in the area you are planning to move to.

Of course, you are entitled to a student loan, but for many people, this just covers the university fees and accommodation, so you will still need money to actually live off. A lot of students work part time, so you will need to consider whether you will have to work around your studies.

The loan amount depends on what your parents earn in a financial year. I was given quite a high student loan and I still struggled to live off of it, as my parents couldn't really afford to help me financially. Of course, they did what they could but I would have never survived without getting a job.

Maintenance loans are available to most students, and these are for costs such as: rent, bills and textbooks. I also had a maintenance grant which is something you don't have to pay back, it just topped my loan up by a couple of extra thousand for the year which just about covered my rent of around £800 a month at the time.

In the last few years, tuition fees for public universities in the UK have risen to as much as £9,000 a year. I started just at the right time before they increased the fees. I paid £3,000 a year, and still walked away with £30,000 worth of debt. I believe these fees are similar to those of public universities in the US.

Students are entitled to borrow up to £7,751 in maintenance loans and £9,000 in tuition fees. On average, somebody taking the maximum loan amount for a 3-year course will expect to have borrowed more than £50,000 by the time they graduate due to the increase in fees.

You don't have to borrow the full amount, but you will receive interest on it as soon as it reaches your bank account. The more you earn, the more interest will be added.

Fees are set to rise again in 2017, along with the "maintenance grant" becoming a "maintenance loan", meaning it will need to be paid back. This increase will be related to the quality of teaching and rankings. It is becoming more difficult for the average person to attend university now, due to financial reasons. I believe employers will recognize this and the importance of someone having a degree won't be so much of a requirement when interviewing candidates for a job position.

JADE MARSH

Things you will be paying for whilst at university:

- Travel to and from university
- Living costs such as bills and food
- Textbooks
- Travel to and from work if you get a job

Can your parents or spouse help you out financially? Overestimate what you will need so that you are covered, in case something else crops up that you didn't account for.

I studied in London, which is one of the most expensive cities in the world to live in, so I had to work part time in a restaurant. This is another thing to consider when choosing universities that are in cities- the cost of living will be more than if you went to a university in a town.

Rent prices in London are very high, and my maintenance loan just about covered my rent, and then any money I earned from the restaurant was for me to buy food and live off of.

A lot of people I knew at university had student overdrafts, so you also need to be careful you don't get yourself in debt with that to cover your living costs.

Having said all of this, there are a large number of people who go to university and they manage to get by, so don't be put off that you won't be able to afford to go. Expect to get into additional debt on top of your student loan if you aren't careful, although it is certainly a good life lesson on how to manage money when you're young.

I actually lived at home for my first and third year and managed to save some of my loan, so there is the benefit of doing that if you go to a university close by.

11. When will I start paying back my loan?

Many people are worried about getting into debt especially as big as the debt you will find yourself in after university. I think this is only worth it if the job you're going for is one you can see yourself doing for life and it is necessary to get a degree for, otherwise, I would never encourage anyone to get into this amount of debt for a job that you could have got without the qualification.

Although this is probably the best debt to be in, as you don't have to start paying it back until you are earning a certain amount. The more you earn, the more you pay back each month. If you stop earning a certain amount, then obviously it goes down again so you don't have the worry of making regular payments a month if you aren't earning enough to cover the repayments. You pay 9% of your income that is over the threshold.

The table below explains the repayment structure of paying back a student loan.

Yearly income before Tax	Monthly Income	Monthly Repayment
Up to £21,000	£1,750	£0
£22,000	£1,833	£7
£25,000	£2,083	£30
£30,000	£2,500	£67
£35,000	£2,916	£105

12. Will the benefits outweigh the costs?

There is no hard evidence that says that having a degree makes you a better quality employee. However, there are some common traits that can be recognized from someone who has a degree.

Graduates have acquired skills that people who don't have one, may not have. Emotional intelligence is one, as by attending a university, especially in a different town or city from where you normally live will give you some good social skills, independence and the ability to work with people who are different from yourself in an environment you are not used to.

This will benefit you in more ways than you know. It's a big deal to start somewhere new on your own, not knowing anyone and having to build relationships with people you live with or are in the same class as you.

This will give you good communication skills; the ability to work with people you wouldn't necessarily be friends with outside of work.

Other skills you will acquire will be the ability to do presentations confidently and speak in front of people, which can be used a lot in the work place depending on what type of job you end up in. You will also have learnt how to write reports, essays and assignments successfully.

You will learn about investment and managing your money as you live on your own. You are committed to investing time and money into yourself and would have stuck at something for 3-4 years, which shows a lot to an employer. It tells them you aren't someone who quits easily when taking on a large commitment, giving you more credibility.

When looking at whether it is worth the investment, that depends really on what you're going for. It is true that graduates are paid more, but then it's also true that a large number of graduates aren't working in a highly paid job because they struggled to find one, which related to their degree, or they decided it wasn't for them after all.

This really depends on the type of degree you are studying for. I have mentioned before that some jobs require one but others, it isn't always a necessity.

If you are going to be working in the creative industry for instance, I don't believe it is worth the investment as it isn't necessary for you to have a degree for this type of industry.

Of course, for some specialised careers, you have no choice but to go and get a degree, therefore it is worth the investment, as you know you're undertaking a specialised subject and training to become an expert on that subject.

13. Is now the right time for me to go?

There is no rush to go to university. The normal process is go to school, then at 16 either stay on to do A-levels or go to college to do them. Then finally going to university at the age of 18.

I personally think your too young straight from college to be making such an important decision as to what you want to do for a full time career. Some people know what they want and that's great, but others have no idea, so they end up studying something that they aren't really interested in, and hence they just go for the sake of going.

Take your time when deciding and figure out if it's the right time for you. If you're unsure, then take time out until you become sure.

The right time is when you know exactly what you want to study and you have researched into what you want to go into. You know exactly what you need, degree wise, experience wise, and you have a clear plan of the path you want to take and what you will do when you graduate.

I would always encourage anyone that studies for a degree, to get as much experience as humanly possible whilst studying. Do not waste the three years on learning just the theory of your chosen subject. Learn the practical side as well; this will make you more employable when you graduate as it can take months to find a job. Again, that's more time that you aren't earning a decent income.

14. How important is getting a degree to me?

It is a big commitment going to university, not just financially but it's a huge time commitment, so it really needs to be something your serious about, not just something you feel you should do, or don't mind doing because you don't have many options. If this is the case, you won't put all the effort in that is required, and it is likely you won't even finish your first year.

New research shows that students of 2016 have already dropped out of university when the New Year started. 27% of refreshers have either dropped out of their course or were contemplating dropping out over the summer. The reasons being that they had either found full time employment because of the expense, not being happy with the course they had chosen, not enjoying the university they were at and being disappointed in further education.

15. Am I going for a party lifestyle or a career?

There are some people who go to university just for the experience like the partying, socializing, living away from home and becoming independent. Although it's good to experience as much as you can in life, there are cheaper alternatives to experience these things without going to university.

The number one reason you should be going is for your career because you are planning on using the degree after you graduate.

What type of experience do you want? A small experience? Or a big experience? It is a good idea to visit each university you apply for to get a good feel for each one. You will be spending 3-4 years of your life there so you want to make sure you choose the university that will suit you best. It is worth investing your time in something that is going to be a big part of your life for the next couple of years.

Although university is a time in your life where you are likely to meet your friends for life and have the best time as you are approaching becoming an adult. It is also a very serious time in the early stages of your career, and it shouldn't be wasted as a time to just have fun.

16. Will going to university land me my dream job?

A degree alone won't land you your dream job; it's ultimately down to you. It is your responsibility to gain as much experience as you can whilst studying and find yourself a job after your studies. It also depends how persistent you are, and whether you have a good work ethic or not. If you work hard, you normally get rewarded for it. You need to stand out from everyone else for any internship you can get after university or if you can land yourself a job first, work as hard as you can and make your degree count.

17. Am I going as a way to put off working full time?

Some people enjoy being a student, so that they can put off going into the real world of work, especially if they are unsure on what they want to do. If that is the case, you're better off going straight into a job as it will help you figure out what you like and what you don't like, and at least you will be earning rather than struggling as a student.

18. How long have I been thinking about going to university?

Is university something you have wanted to do for as long as you can remember? For some people, it has always been part of the plan, especially if their parents went and so did their other family members.

19. If I don't go, will I regret it?

There isn't a time limit on when you can attend university. You can go at any age, so if you do regret not going, it's never too late, so don't rush into it thinking you only have one chance to go.

Age is just a number when it comes to higher education. The number of mature (over 21) university applicants in the UK has steadily risen over the past few years. There has been a 15% rise in 21-24 year olds, and over 17% in over 25 year olds since 2008.

20. How do I apply?

All applications made to UK universities are made through the UCAS website, www.ucas.com There is a deadline, so make sure you get your application in on time, all the information can be found on the site.

21. How do I deal with my family's disappointment if I decide not to go?

- Keep calm
- Know your argument
- Do your research

Telling your parents you don't want to go to university can be daunting especially if they are adamant on you going. If you have another plan other than university, then it is likely they will understand. I think some parents won't take it well if their child decides they don't want to go but doesn't have any other plans in place, as then they would probably worry about what you're going to do with your life.

You aren't going to please your family every time you make an important life decision. Growing up is your chance to make your own choices and mistakes. It's all part of the learning process in becoming an adult. You need to trust your instinct, once you have done all the relevant research.

It's your life, no one else can tell you how you how to live it. You have to remember that your parents only want what is best for you, so their negativity if they have any, is coming from a good place, as they just want to see you do well.

The next chapter will help you in making your final decision in deciding what the next step is for your career and future.

CHAPTER 4

Making a clear decision

Now, you have asked yourself all the questions needed in making your final decision. You have weighed up the pros and cons, it is now time to actually make a decision. If you are like me, this could take a while. I am, or was one of the most indecisive people. Now, I make decisions a lot quicker. I think it's easier as you get older and wiser, you trust your own instincts through experiences you may have had or your own knowledge.

Where we end up in life is based on the decisions and choices we make on a daily basis. Where you are today is the result of the decisions and choices you have made in the past.

So whatever decision you make, think about where you might be in 3 years. If you decide to go to university, you will be about to graduate and think about what you might plan to do.

Where will you be in 3 years if you don't go to university? You will probably be working either for someone else or yourself. Imagine your life both ways and then see how you feel emotionally and physically.

- **What does each path look like to you?**

- **How do they make you feel?**

- **Which one feels more positive?**

- **Which one feels more negative?**

Remember, whatever decision you do make doesn't mean you are stuck with the decision for life. It will have an impact on you either positively or negatively; you won't know this until a couple of years. If you have looked at the pros and cons and compared each one to what you want to do now, what you feel is right for you and no one else, then you can only do your best in your current situation, you can't get everything right.

Life is about learning and making mistakes, as long as you feel sure and confident in what you decide today, then that is all that matters. You deal with the consequences later; if there are any.

No one knows you better than you know yourself. You can only ever rely on your natural instinct, so you better get used to using it.

Make your decision, stick with it and be confident. How does your body feel when you think about it months down the line?

It's ok to do the opposite of society and make a different choice to your friends and what people might be encouraging you to do.

The world's richest 1% of the population, owns 50% of the world's wealth. This is no accident. This group of people; the minority of the population set out to do things differently to the average person, so they could live a better quality of life. They were not afraid to take risks and do things differently to everyone else around them.

I was given some great advice once, which was "Listen to the people whose life you want rather than the people whose life you don't want".

It is important to ask yourself questions on a daily basis to find out how you truly feel. Writing down your answers is key, as you may find that you will just keep writing and you will be surprised at what may be written down. Our minds are full of thousands of thoughts a day; the average person has between 50,000 and 70,000 a day! That is a lot of thoughts, which most of them you likely don't take much notice of.

Sometimes, it's hard to translate how we truly feel, as we over think things and struggle to make basic decisions on a daily basis.

Our thoughts are clogged up by what we hear from others, and we may change our minds due to other people's opinions and influences without even knowing it.

Have you ever felt an emotion or feeling and then told yourself to stop thinking about it? Sometimes, its easy to control our thoughts, but other times they get the better of us and we can lose control of them, resulting in us getting emotional or angry or even confused. It is important to acknowledge as many of our thoughts as we can, as it may help us figure out any problems or challenges we may be going through. Our minds are so clever, so make a habit of listening to them and what we say to ourselves.

It's like permanent rush hour in our brains; it's no wonder we lose touch with ourselves. This equates to 35-48 thoughts per minute per person, this amount of overcrowding in our minds prevents us from seeing things clearly and identifying how we truly feel.

A way to control the mass amount of thoughts we have is by meditating. Meditation can help control your mind, and the amount of thoughts you think. It allows you to think of specific thoughts rather than everything at once. It can help you listen to your instincts more clearly.

It is great for depression and anxiety and can have some real benefits, like sharpening your concentration. It gives you time to create, solve problems, come up with new ideas, and think clearer about things you don't always have the time for.

It is a chance for you to take time out for yourself and hear your own voice clearly and connect with your inner self on a deeper level than what you normally would.

The way to meditate is by simply taking some time out to relax your body and mind. It is up to you how long you meditate for, it could be 5 minutes, 20 minutes or even an hour, you decide. So you can sit down in an upright position, close your eyes if you prefer, you could listen to some soothing music, it's really up to you. Just take time to concentrate on your breathing and you might be surprised at the thoughts you think.

Concentrate on something, so it could be one thought or one decision you have been trying to make and you haven't really had the time to think it through properly. Or you could concentrate on nothing and just let your mind think freely.

It can be quite difficult at first, as we are used to juggling our thoughts on a daily basis when making decisions, worrying about something and making judgements. It might take a couple of attempts to take control of your mind fully and stop it from wandering, but the more you do it, the better you will become. Persevere with it, and you will start to notice the benefits.

When you have made your decision, ask yourself these 4 questions to confirm you have made the right choice.

1. Does this align with my short-term goals?
2. What is guiding my decision, mind or heart?
3. Does my decision line up with my values?
4. Can I logically and honestly defend my decision?

By now, you should have looked at the pros and cons, and you have asked yourself 21 of the most important questions when it comes to making the decision for or against university for you.

Now, only you can make the decision, listen to others advice but ultimately, listen to your own voice.

Finally, and perhaps most importantly, once you have made a decision, stick with it, and don't waste your time thinking about "What ifs". Accept the decision you have made and move on. If it is the wrong one, then so be it. You can deal with that after. Or it could be the best decision you have ever made.

CHAPTER 5

What should I do instead of get a degree?

As I have already explained in this book, a degree isn't your only option if you want to obtain a great job and become a success in what you desire.

Always research into what your options are when looking at doing anything in life; never just go with the first option in case you can find a better one.

A degree isn't the only thing that will set you apart from others; it's all about how you carry yourself and how proactive you are when looking for opportunities.

Some alternatives of going to university:

1.) Study:

You should always be learning in life; that should never stop. If you aren't learning, you may as well be dead. You can pretty much learn anything you want to these days from YouTube, so if there is something you are interested in teaching yourself, its more than likely you have free access to it online.

When we are learning, we are growing, so you should dedicate yourself to lifelong learning; knowledge is the fundamental source of value in today's world. Consistently learning is the number one way to overcome any obstacles that might stand in front of you on your road to success.

As Tony Robbins says "People are rewarded in public on what they do in private". Knowledge is power; it's what separates you from others and allows you to stand out as an expert in your chosen field.

As long as you are continually learning, you will always be ahead in what you choose to do; never miss an opportunity to learn and grow.

There is a lot to be learned from the world around you, rather than sitting in a classroom. The best way to learn is by doing not just by being shown. It also depends what type of learner you are.

Everyone learns differently and has a different style, which one is you?

Decide from the list below…

Visual:

If you are a visual learner, then you prefer to learn using pictures, diagrams, images, colors and mind-maps.

Physical:

If you are a physical learner, then you will learn the best by actually doing. You're physically using your body to support you when learning. This is definitely me; I much prefer to be shown something and then I do. I learn quicker this way and retain information better, rather than being shown something visually.

Logical:

If you are a logical learner, then you learn best by using systems and reasoning. You need concepts explained to you, so you can understand the reasons behind what is being taught and you have a clearer picture of what it is all about.

I would say that this style of learning reflects me slightly too, as sometimes I am not just content with being told something. I like to know why and how it works, so I can grasp the full extent of what I am being taught.

Verbal:

If you are a verbal learner, then you prefer to learn using words, and saying things out loud. You would do this both in speech and writing when taking information in.

Aural:

If you are an aural learner, then you choose to learn using sounds, like music, rhythms, and recordings.

Solitary:

If you are a solitary learner, then you prefer to be on your own and learn through self-study. This is a great way to learn if you are entrepreneurial because it is likely you will have to self-teach to get things done, so you can learn quickly and not rely on others to teach you.

Social:

If you are a social learner, then you enjoy working with others, in groups. Your goal is to work with others as much as possible.

It's likely you will fall into one or more of these categories and sometimes, all of them at one stage in your life, depending on the type of learning that is occurring.

Learn life skills we don't get taught in school/university:

- How to handle money
- Communication
- Building relationships with people
- Time management
- Personal development
- Finding a job

Learn about failure:

Thomas Edison, the inventor of the light bulb, saw failure in a positive way; he made 1000 unsuccessful attempts when inventing the light bulb. When asked how he felt about failing 1000 times, his response was… "I didn't fail 1000 times, the light bulb was an invention with a 1000 steps".

If you look at the most successful people in life, they had many failures before they became successful, it's just a lot of people don't see what it took for them to get there, they only see their triumphs.

Another example is Henry Ford, the inventor of 'FORD' cars; he went bankrupt and failed five times before succeeding.

The formula to success is failure… so next time you fail at something, remember you are one step closer to succeeding.

Instead of looking at your failed attempts as failure, look at it as a way of life, and as an opportunity to learn. It is something you have to get used to; the quicker you can overcome failure, the quicker you will become successful.

Learn about your health and exercise:

The older you get, the more you become aware of how important your health is, and it baffles me that we aren't taught this properly at school. Especially with the obesity issues we have in today's society.

We should be teaching ourselves about the processed foods that are easily available to us on a daily basis. We shouldn't trust everything we can pick up at the supermarket. This is another book in itself, so I won't go into too much detail, but your body is just as important as your mind, and so we have to look after it. Putting the right foods into our body will make us feel more energised, more positive and motivated.

We should all be doing some form of exercise daily, even if it is low intensity. Not enough people see the importance of this, but it can also have a positive effect on your mood and attitude, which in turn will make you perform better in your daily life.

It is down to you to use your initiative and don't wait to be taught things. Go out and teach yourself, you can ask pretty much anything on Google these days and you will get an answer.

You need to treat your body with respect, so you can live a healthy and fulfilling life.

2) Get a job

In reality, I should have just applied for jobs until I eventually got an interview. It might be hard to start with without a degree, but the idea is to stick out to employers.

When applying for a position, you are likely to be up against a large number of people who may be more qualified than you.

Without a degree, you need to think of other ways to impress the employer. You have to be different and stand out. Visit the company your looking into and ask to speak to the manager. Face to face is a lot more effective, give them your CV and explain your reasons for not attending university.

Be honest with them, it is likely they won't have a position for you straight away but they may be able to offer you something, or they can keep your CV on file. Already, you have made a great impression as you have used your initiative to get what you want. This will make you stand out from the crowd. Be persistent without being pushy, the more you show commitment and the desire to want to work somewhere, the more chance you have of being heard.

A university degree doesn't guarantee success, but not having one doesn't set you up for failure either.

3) Start a business

You can pretty much earn money from anything these days, especially with the Internet. Kids, are making money from YouTube videos, playing computer games, blogging, vlogging, the list goes on.

Find something your good at or you're interested in. If you want to be in control of your future and be your own boss, then starting your own business is the way forward. It has never been a better time to become an entrepreneur, as the future will see more and more people create their own income streams, as technology replaces jobs.

With so much free value and content online, you can teach yourself to build any successful business you desire, as there will have been someone else who has done it before you.

It's all about learning from people who are where you want to be, don't try and reinvent the wheel; it will just take you longer than is necessary to become a success.

Many people are put off by being an entrepreneur because they see it as an unstable career. Most people need the security of a job knowing they are going to get paid each month and knowing how much. Although in today's economy, no job is safe. I would much rather be in control of my finances and build my own dream, rather than help build someone else's.

You could also get a full time job to pay the bills and then start a business on the side, which is what a lot of people to do to start with so it takes the pressure off paying the bills.

Another reason people are put off becoming an entrepreneur is failure. Failure isn't a bad thing. Success doesn't exist without failure, and so you may have to fail a number of times in order to succeed at what you're doing.

4) Go travelling

Don't feel pressured into making one of the most important decisions of your life. Why not take a year out and go travelling? Go "find yourself".

A gap year can look impressive on your CV nowadays, especially if you work whilst travelling. It shows cultural awareness and the ability to work independently, plus I think it says a lot about one's personality too.

If you do look to take a year out, make the most of it and go abroad. Some people take a year out and work in a low paid job where they live. This is fine if it is what you choose to do. It's better than rushing into university if you're unsure, but wouldn't you like to make the most of your year out? See the world, meet new people; you never know what opportunities will come your way. Always be keen to experience new things as your only young once.

It is also a great way to learn. You will certainly grow up from travelling as it will force you to depend on yourself and survive without your parents. You will come back older and wiser with more life experience than you left… that's if you decide to come back!

It doesn't have to be a year; it could be 6 months or even less. Even taking a holiday can be beneficial, as by removing yourself from your daily environment, it can open up your eyes to what else is out there and might make you think differently about what you want to do. I always feel extremely motivated when I go away on holiday. It always puts a spring in my step and helps me make important decisions as it's good to get a clear mind and take yourself out of your comfort zone for a short period of time.

There is no rush to start a career at the age of 22, which is when a lot of students graduate, after going straight to college from high school, and then straight to university from college. Of course, some people choose to go to university later on in life, but the majority are young adults.

What is the rush to start a career so young? I started my hairdressing career at 16. I then decided I wanted a new career, so went to university at 21. I then started my own business at 24, that didn't work out, so I started another business at 26. You will find this is quite common, as some people try one thing out, it doesn't work, so they try something else out and so on.

The average person has at least 6 different careers in their life, so don't be surprised if you decide on one career and then change it to another, it's completely normal. Therefore, it's good to try out different options before deciding on one.

There really is no rush, obviously if you can find your passion in life from a young age, it's got to be a real benefit to you, but the point I am trying to make is, don't rush into university if it's not something you are sure of as you don't need to have figured everything out by the age of 22.

I have always thought it was quite odd to have to know what you want to do with your life when you leave school. It's a question that gets asked a lot as you come to the end of high school. I think most students have no clue what they want to do, because until you have experienced life and working in the real world, done some travelling, met some inspiring people, how are you supposed to know what you want to do?

5) Traineeships

A traineeship is a work placement, where you can learn what is expected in the work place. You must be between 16-24 years old and they last between 6 weeks to 6 months.

At the end of the placement, if there are any jobs available, you should receive an interview for the job.

6) Apprenticeships

An apprenticeship is a real job with training provided; you learn and earn whilst studying for your qualifications. They can take up to 1-4 years depending on what you are learning.

You can get an apprenticeship in 170 different industries now and have the choice of 1400 different job roles. Some of those include, hairdresser, dental nurse, trainee accountant and cabin crew.

As you can see, there are plenty of other options in life than just going down the degree route. Don't waste your life taking on a big commitment like I did when I was unsure. Use your initiative and seek out all the information that is readily available for you to make a wise choice, based on your values and beliefs of what direction you want your working life to go in. There is no rush, so take your time and choose accordingly to what best suits you.

The next chapter will help you follow your passion in life, which should highlight more to you on whether university is the right choice for you or not.

CHAPTER 6

Finding your passion

It can be frustrating when people say to you… "Follow your passion!" and you have no idea what that is. How do you know if you are passionate about something? The truth is that it's natural for everyone to be passionate about something, even if we don't know what that passion is yet. Working on something we love adds more meaning to our lives, and gives us more of a purpose.

Passions can develop later on in life, especially if they are just hobbies, and its likely they will change as you mature.

The type of passion I am encouraging you to explore is one you can make a living from.

Once you develop a passion, you can then develop a way of making an income from it rather than just working at a job that you don't enjoy, as that can be soul destroying. How would it feel if you were waking up each day to work on something that you loved and kept you excited about life?

Personal development is the most important thing for you to focus on when you are trying to figure out what your passion is. It will allow you to get deep within yourself and find out who you really are and what motivates you.

We all want to make money right? And live a nice life, but unfortunately that isn't enough. We all need to find our purpose to feel truly happy and know what we were put on this earth to do. We need to serve people through what we learn and what we can teach, adding value to as many lives as possible.

Some popular passions include music, sports, dance, business, food, exercise and travel. I believe if you are following your true passion, you will lead a more fulfilled life.

When trying to figure out what your passion in life is, ask yourself these two questions:

1. If time and money were no object, how would I really enjoy spending my life?

2. What do I desire?

Your main focus shouldn't be on making money when discovering what your passion is. If you are just chasing the money, you will spend your life doing things you don't like doing just to live.

If it is your true passion, you can always find a way to make an income from it once you have become a master of it. People will pay you a lot of money if you are a master in your field.

Everyone is interested in something. You might not know it yet, but you will discover it if you open your mind and search for it.

A lot of people are too scared to follow their passion in life, as they are more concerned with finding a job that generates a regular income to pay the bills. Although that is vital, why not follow your passion alongside that, you never know in the future, it may result in a career for you.

Don't live the same life as your parents, friends, or your grandparents if that isn't what you want to do, as you will just be living based on someone else's values and beliefs, and it won't make you happy. You have to ultimately go for what it is you want in life.

Here are ways to help you discover your passion:

1.) Have the right attitude:

Finding your passion begins with a mind-set. Imagine you walked into a restaurant and said "I am not hungry" and you took an instant disliking. You are already setting yourself up to not like anything, and it is likely you won't find anything you want to eat as you have walked in with a bad attitude, expecting the worse.

By default, most of us prefer the negative mind-set unfortunately. It is natural for us to have negative thoughts, as we are constantly surrounded by negativity in our environment and the situations we face on a daily basis. This is due to the people we come into contact with and bad past experiences, which all contribute to our pessimistic perspective.

It becomes like a daily habit, and we don't even know we are doing it. This is why it is important to always surround yourself with uplifting people, and ignore all the awful things that are going on in the world. Once you start to shift your negative thoughts to positive ones, it will be life changing for you. It will help you deal with challenges and stressful situations more successfully. It is all about your state of mind, and it's up to you how you choose to feel about something.

Once you focus on the lessons you learn from any negative situation that you are put in, it automatically changes the way you feel about it to a more positive feeling. By doing this, it can be life changing for you.

This golden rule applies when your searching for your passion; if you think it will be hard, then it will be, if you think you will never find your passion, then you won't find it. If you don't believe your passion exists, then how do you expect to find it? You will become closed minded to any sign or possibility that may come your way.

I never expected to find my passion, as I was concentrating too much on making money. Once you remove that objective from your mind, you are open to what you actually should be doing. Again, I reiterate any chance you have the opportunity to do something you wouldn't normally do, jump at the chance!

Meet new people, do new things as this will inspire you and you never know your passion may lie behind it.

"You are the average of the five people you spend the most time with." – Jim Rohn

The best way to become what you want and do what you want is to surround yourself with the people that have already done it, and the people who are working on their passions on a daily basis. The more you can get yourself around those people who you aspire to be, the more you become and think like those people. Being with likeminded individuals, is the best way for you to experience having a breakthrough.

I am living proof of that. Being around some of the most inspiring and ambitious people at the retreat was life changing for me. It completely changed the way I thought and allowed me to discover my passion. I came home more confident, more sure of what I wanted out of life, and made some great connections and lifelong friends.

2.) Slow down, keep it simple and have fun:

Don't let it overwhelm and stress you out. It may take a while for you to find your passion, or you could be worried that you don't have one. I was worried because I didn't think I was ever truly passionate about anything, but once you slow down and tap into the best version of yourself, its likely you will find the answers you have been searching for. To do this, you should incorporate one or more of exercise, yoga, meditation, walking, anything that will get you to zone out and have some quiet time with yourself.

3.) Write:

Writing can be extremely useful. Once you wake up in the morning, you should start writing as much as you can, and don't even think about what you are writing and see what develops on the paper. You may be inspired by something that you hadn't given much thought about.

4.) Find your excitement and follow it:

There must be one or more things that excite you, so work out what they are and do it. Then follow it once you have found your next excitement, do the same and follow it again. Sometimes, it's hard to remember what has excited us in the past or what excites us now.

5.) Focus on a topic:

Pick a topic you enjoy such as:

- Art
- Music
- Fashion
- Sports
- Travel
- Business

Think about what truly inspires and interests you, whatever excites you will lead you to your passion. You may already be doing something you are passionate about but you don't know it yet, especially if you are already working. When its labelled as a "job", it takes away the passion you may have felt when you first started.

You need to push past the fear. We all fear change and doing something that we might not have necessarily done before, but it's good to feel uneasy as it means you are pushing yourself out of your comfort zone. Don't settle in a job you hate, or is mediocre, as that will make you miserable.

You deserve to find what truly motivates you and share it with people. Don't be afraid to go and search for it, or allow yourself to become passionate about something.

It may take a while, but I guarantee you there is something inside of you that will ignite your fire, you just need to be confident enough to explore it.

6.) Look for the clues:

Now, it's time to think about past experiences, anything that you can remember that made you happy. Think about the situation and think about what it truly meant to you. Why did you enjoy it? Did you serve as a leader? Did you help someone in some way? Did you perform a certain activity, which you think you could do full time?

When you first acknowledge what your interests are, they might at first seem disconnected, but you may be able to work out a passion by incorporating a couple of them or at least using one. How can you then create a career from it?

I have always enjoyed teaching people, and was told when I was hairdressing that I was good at teaching others. I like to make whatever I am teaching really simple and save my clients time by giving them as much information and support possible, so they don't waste their time figuring it out for themselves. That is what I believe a good mentor does, it is not about doing the work for someone, but assisting them in the best way possible.

I enjoy teaching and I know I am good at it, so it makes sense when I look back now that I should have gone into a coaching career, as that is my strength.

To be able to support people in becoming the best version of themselves is so rewarding and I love being able to make a difference in people's lives, just like people have in mine.

I hope this helps in finding your passion. Remember, it might be a process that will take a while, but it's important that you are constantly being pro-active and you are ready to accept anything that comes your way.

You have to be committed to finding your passion and become the best person you can be through personal development, and in return, your passion will present itself to you in one or more ways when you are ready to accept it.

Be ready and be excited, you deserve to find it and work with it if that's what you choose to do; the world needs your passion.

CHAPTER 7

The next step: Finding a mentor

Now you have figured out what your passion is, or you are on the way to finding out what it is, the next step is to find a mentor, someone you can collaborate with.

It can be very daunting going it alone and it's always good to have someone else there who knows what he or she is doing, to help you, and it is useful to have someone to bounce ideas off of.

Your desire to succeed can be extremely overwhelming, especially when you don't know where to start. Working with a mentor is important when you want to become successful, as they know how to get what you want, so they can show you, rather than you making all the mistakes and figuring it out for yourself, which will be a long and painful process.

The benefits of having a mentor is to have someone that inspires you to be better and wake up each day and make a difference.

No successful person got to where they are today without having someone there to guide them to where they are, as it isn't possible to become your best version without outsourcing some help.

Having a mentor, holds you accountable, which is the number one key to success I believe. Most people will fail at anything if they don't have someone there to hold them accountable. If your friend is trying their best to lose weight, and one week they come to you and say "I don't want to go to the gym tonight, I would rather stay in and get a takeaway". As a friend, you would normally say, "Go on do it, you deserve it" what you should be doing is holding them accountable for what they set out to do.

There are so many distractions in life, and it can be easy to neglect certain tasks or take the easy option when we feel like it. If you have someone to answer to, it keeps you focused and more motivated to complete whatever you need to do.

You need to borrow someone's belief in you, until you can start to believe in yourself. A mentor is there to guide you on the right path, to give you confidence and see greatness in you, even if you can't see it in yourself.

We all need a mentor in life. We start off with our parents, then go to school and our teachers become our mentors, and then when we leave education, then what? Who mentors us then? I think this is one of the biggest mistakes we make, we should have some kind of mentor throughout our whole life.

Whether it is a mentor to help us in our relationship, our marriage, at work, a business mentor, a life coach, someone who teaches us how to raise our children. Our mentors come in the form of friends and family, but are they qualified enough to give us the right advice? Sometimes yes, sometimes no. What if they are mentoring us in a way that suits them? I am not saying they are doing something wrong by doing this, but it helps to have someone on the outside that can see things in you that people in your inner circle might not see.

I also think that sometimes it means more hearing from someone you don't know about how good you are at something, than it does from someone you know, as people that know you can be "biased". If someone you don't know picks up on your good qualities and strengths, you take it in more and accept it more than if you hear it from close friends and family who are supposed to love you and see the good in you.

The various types of mentors you have throughout your life:

Growing up, your first mentor/mentors are inevitably your parents. From birth, they teach you, or should have taught you how to walk, talk, eat, table manners, how to swim, tie a shoe lace, communicate, interact socially, respect others (especially your elders), how to laugh, how to cry, how to have fun, how to make friends, the list goes on.

I remember growing up thinking everything my parents said was right, and that every opinion or value of theirs was correct; I believed they knew it all.

Once I got a bit older and I was connecting with other people, I realised I had different values and opinions to my parents, this was through experiencing things they hadn't or learning from other people. This isn't a bad thing and is normal, but I now have my own beliefs and core values which are different to what my parents think, so of course, there will be others out there who can influence me in different ways, this doesn't mean they can influence me in a better way, it's just in a different way.

It is vital you learn from as many different people as you can, and experience as many different experiences as you can, as this will have a huge benefit on your life.

This will provide you with the tools and skills you need to live a much more productive and fulfilling life. Learning new life skills will help you understand the world around you, clearer serving you in finding ways to survive challenges that life will inescapably throw at you.

At a point in your adult life, you will outgrow your parent's advice and it will become less valid as you learn new things that they might not know, and you have people around you who are more accustomed to your way of thinking in life or your career.

Then you move onto school, the next stage in your life, your mentors then become your teachers, and your friends. We are influenced by the people who come into our lives, whether that is positively or negatively.

When looking for a professional mentor the top qualities you should look for are:

- **A mentor who delivers value to people for nothing in return**

Your mentor should be someone who is giving out constant value for free. This will also show what type of person they are, that they genuinely want to help people, and have their best interests at heart. That it isn't just about making money for them, it is about making an impact in the world.

- **A mentor who is eager to communicate their knowledge, skills and expertise**

Rather than keeping what they know to themselves, good mentors are willing to share all they know and more. They take the relationship between the two of you very seriously and are willing to invest their time and commitment in helping you continually.

- **A mentor you look up to and respect as a role model who exhibits a positive mental attitude**

A good mentor for you is someone who exposes themselves as a role model through their success. They always demonstrate the qualities it takes to be successful and show you what is needed in order for you to become the best in your field.

- **A mentor who sees the importance in continued learning and growth, so they can be the best mentor to you possible**

Anyone that thinks they don't need to learn anymore and they know all there is to know, is someone you don't want to work with. A mentor who sees the importance in always staying up to date with the latest trends and always willing to better himself or herself is someone you want to work with. They can't help you, unless they are at the best level they can be. There is always something new to learn, no one knows it all. Good mentors are committed to always striving for the next level and taking you with them. Continued learning also keeps them motivated and passionate about what they do.

- **A mentor who is passionate about their work, giving value to people, and is genuine and authentic**

You want to work with someone who not only enjoys what they do, but also is extremely passionate about their work. If they are not, then they won't be passionate about helping you succeed. Someone who inspires and motivates you to always be better, someone who is authentic and knows their self-worth in their field. You don't want to work with someone who is still establishing himself or herself as an expert.

- **A mentor who has a personal interest in you and building a professional relationship with you**

You want to work with someone who wants the success for you as much as you do for yourself. Someone who genuinely cares and has a personal interest in you and not just looking to take your money from you.

- **A mentor you actually like and can see yourself working well with**

You will be working very closely with this person, so you need to be able to get on with them and be able to build a working relationship, otherwise this could affect your business in a negative way. Not everyone is cut out to work together; there might be a clash of personalities.

A good mentor for you should have either achieved what you are looking to accomplish, or have knowledge on how to do it, and have helped someone before you achieve it, otherwise why would you listen to them?

- **A mentor who can provide you with support and also be able to give you constructive criticism when necessary.**

A good mentor is someone who can build you up and see more in you than you can to start with, but they also need to be able to give you constructive criticism if needed. You need someone that can be completely honest with you and tell you when you are doing something wrong, or you need to improve in certain areas. Without this, you will never get better or learn from your mistakes, and grow into being the right person you need to be in order to succeed.

- **A mentor who is respected by others and successful in their field**

You want to work with someone who is well known in the industry you are in, as collaboration is so important. Collaboration is the fundamental reason for someone's success, as the more successful people you can connect and work with, the more reputable you will become. Those people will also offer value and advice to you, which can be life changing in itself.

For success, one's ability and experience are less valuable and less significant than one's association with the right people.

- **A mentor who is approachable, friendly and is a good listener**

You want someone who you can easily talk to and you don't feel intimidated by; someone who you can go to if you have problem. Having said that they aren't your counsellor, so don't dump all your personal problems on them, only business related ones.

When you have found your mentor, there are qualities you should adopt too. These include:

- **The willingness to learn and be coachable**

There is no point paying for someone to advise you and then you ignore what they tell you and do it your own way anyway. Don't be the person who thinks they know it all, or who thinks, "I don't have to do it like that, I'll do it my way". Remember they know more than you, as they have already done what you are trying to do.

- **Be pro-active and use your own initiative**

Put into action what you have been advised to do straight away. The worst thing for a mentor is when they are coaching someone and that person isn't prepared to do what he or she is being told. The mentor will stop working with you as it reflects badly on them and they have their reputation to protect. It is also incredibly frustrating giving up their time on someone who isn't committed to making a change even if you are paying them.

An ethical mentor will also tell you they won't work with you if they genuinely don't think you have it in you to make whatever it is you are working towards, work. It would be wrong for them to take money off of you, knowing you will never succeed at what your trying to succeed at, if you aren't willing to take their advice and put the work in.

- **Be respectful of their time**

You should respect your mentor's time. If you have a coaching session planned with them, make sure you don't mess them around and cancel last minute because you can't be bothered or something seemed more appealing.

They are giving up their time to help you, and remember without them, you won't get to where you want to be. Always respect them and their time, and stay professional.

Conclusion

I wrote this book because I needed guidance when I decided to go to university, and I didn't have someone to give me the advice or knowledge to help me make the best decision at the time. Because of that, I made a huge mistake and it delayed me from creating my ideal lifestyle.

Although it wasn't the best option for me, it was a huge learning curve and was my motivation for writing this book.

I don't want other people to make the same mistake I did. You only live once and life is short. Those 3 years I lost, I won't get it back and I really hope this book has impacted others similar to myself and given them the confidence when it comes to making the right decision.

As I have mentioned, I do think university is necessary for those people who are looking to work in a job that requires specific skills and training. Other than that, I believe it is a time stealer and there are better things you could be doing with your time.

You should now know what type of person you are and what type of life you hope to create for yourself from reading this book. I hope it has given you more clarity on what you want to do in your future and whether you think university is your next best step or not.

My advice to you…

If you know 100% what you want to do in life and you are committed and it requires a degree, then go and get one. I think it would be the best decision for you because a degree can really help you excel in life, dependent on what you want to do.

If you are a little unsure, then why not take a year out? Don't rush into such a big commitment; because once you are there, you are committed to it for 3 years. You don't want to go and then quit after your first year, it will be a waste of money, time and knowing you have failed at something isn't a positive experience and it may hold you back from doing anything else in the future.

If you are an entrepreneur or you want to become one, start today! Don't go to university and delay your success, as it doesn't happen overnight, so you may as well make a start sooner rather than later.

I wish you the best of luck in whatever you decide. Ultimately, it is down to you to create the life of your dreams. People can show you how and support you, but they can't do it for you.

Make the most of any opportunity, build as many relationships and connections with different types of people where ever you go, as you never know when they might come in handy one day! Life has a funny way of guiding you in certain directions at which may seem pointless to you at the time, but it will all add up and make sense to you when you look back.

Work with Jade

My ultimate goal when writing this book was to make an impact in as many peoples lives as possible. I am truly passionate about that and I would love to hear from you. I would appreciate any feedback you can give. Any break through you may have experienced from the result of reading this, or if in any way this book may have helped you or anyone you know, please tell me about it.

Are you ready to create your dream lifestyle?

If you are looking for more support with deciding your next best career step and you want to delve a bit deeper, then look no further!

Contact me today to apply for a free 30-minute consultation and you will also get exclusive access to our private Facebook group. This is a platform for everyone to get encouragement, support, build relationships and receive guidance and support on your next career move.

I have created a 6-week self-study course, which includes 6 course modules, weekly exercises to complete and practical step-by-step guides in helping you discover your purpose in life resulting in you finding a career that you love.

For more information on my 6-week course or one to one coaching, visit **www.jademarsh.com**

For access to our Facebook group find us under the name of **"Get clear on your career"** or copy the link below into your Internet browser.

https://www.facebook.com/groups/714620975354887/

You can also contact me directly through my personal email **jade@jademarsh.com**

Please do not hesitate to get in contact, as I would love to hear from you!

References

Chapter 1:

Allen, K. (2015). UK graduates are wasting degrees in lower-skilled jobs. [online] The Guardian. Available at: https://www.theguardian.com/business/2015/aug/19/uk-failed-create-enough-high-skilled-jobs-graduates-student-debt-report [Accessed 1st September 2016]

Allen, K. (2013). Half of recent UK graduates stuck in non-graduate jobs, says ONS. [online] The Guardian. Available at:https://www.theguardian.com/business/2013/nov/19/half-recent-uk-graduates-stuck-jobs-ons [Accessed 10th August 2016]

(2016). Simon Cowell Biography [online] Bio.com. Available at: http://www.biography.com/people/simon-cowell-10073482#early-career [Accessed: 12th September 2016]

(2016). Richard Branson biography [online] Bio.com. Available at: http://www.biography.com/people/richard-branson-9224520#business-expansion [Accessed: 12th September 2016]

Clark, T. and Ping Chan, S. (2014). A history of Tesco: The rise of Britain's biggest supermarket [online] The Telegraph. Available at: http://www.telegraph.co.uk/finance/markets/2788089/A-history-of-Tesco-The-rise-of-Britains-biggest-supermarket.html [Accessed 16th September 2016]

Kollewe, J. (2012). How Tesco became Britain's no.1 retailer [online] Aol.com. Available at:
http://money.aol.co.uk/2012/03/05/how-tesco-became-britains-no-1-retailer/ [Accessed 16th September 2016]

Chapter 2:

Hemmings, C (2014). Understanding student loans: How exactly do they work? [online] BBC News. Available at:
http://www.bbc.co.uk/newsbeat/article/28418590/understanding-student-loans-how-exactly-do-they-work [Accessed 16th September 2016]

Chapter 3:

Dill, K. (2014). 10 Jobs in high demand that require a college degree [online] Forbes.com. Available at:

http://www.forbes.com/sites/kathryndill/2014/12/01/10-jobs-in-high-demand-that-require-a-bachelors-degree/#733cea1e2adb [Accessed: 12th September 2016]

(2012). 20 great jobs without a college degree [online] Careerscast.com. Available at:

http://www.careercast.com/jobs-rated/20-great-jobs-without-college-degree [Accessed: 3rd September 2016]

Pells, R. (2016). Student tuition fees set to rise as Government unveils white paper university teaching reforms [online] Independent. Available at:

http://www.independent.co.uk/news/education/education-news/student-tuition-fees-set-to-rise-as-government-unveils-university-teaching-reforms-a7030671.html [Accessed: 10th August 2016]

Student loan repayment [online] Student loans company. Available at: http://www.studentloanrepayment.co.uk/portal/page?_pageid=93,6678784&_dad=portal&_schema=PORTAL [Accessed 3rd September 2016]

Ali, A. (2016). Almost a third of first-year students have either already dropped out of university or are thinking of leaving in the summer, survey finds [online] Independent. Available at:http://www.independent.co.uk/student/news/almost-a-third-of-first-year-students-have-either-already-dropped-out-of-university-or-are-thinking-a6807406.html [Accessed: 10th August 2016]

Lacey, H. (2009). Olden times: University for the mature student [online] The Guardian. Available at:https://www.theguardian.com/education/2009/aug/20/clearing-university-mature-students [Accessed: 10th August 2016]

Chapter 4:

Shin, L. (2014). The 85 richest people in the world have as much wealth as the 3.5 billion poorest [online] Forbes. Available at:http://www.forbes.com/sites/laurashin/2014/01/23/the-85-richest-people-in-the-world-have-as-much-wealth-as-the-3-5-billion-poorest/#7dd5f87f324b [Accessed 10th August 2016]

Davis, B. (2013). There are 50,000 thoughts standing between you and your partner every day! [online] The Huffington Post. Available at:
http://www.huffingtonpost.com/bruce-davis-phd/healthy-relationships_b_3307916.html [Accessed: 8th August 2016]

Chapter 5:

Verma, E. (2011). At your fingertips: The 8 types of learning styles [online] Skills you need. Available at:
http://www.skillsyouneed.com/rhubarb/fingerprints-learning-styles.html [Accessed 2nd September 2016]

Wenk, G. (2010). How does food affect our brain? [online] Psychology today. Available at:
https://www.psychologytoday.com/blog/your-brain-food/201010/how-does-food-affect-our-brain [Accessed 2nd September 2016]

(2016) Apprenticeships and traineeships. [online] National career service. Available at:
https://nationalcareersservice.direct.gov.uk/youngpeople/Pages/apprenticeshipstraineeships/traineeships.aspx [Accessed 3rd September 2016]

www.ingramcontent.com/pod-product-compliance
Lightning Source LLC
Chambersburg PA
CBHW070253190526
45169CB00001B/393